Egypt's Ancient Secrets

VALLEY OF THE
GOLDEN MUMMIES

A Giant Cemetery

by Ruth Owen

Consultant: Dr. Angela McDonald
Subject Specialist and University Teacher—Archaeology, Classics, and Egyptology
Centre for Open Studies, University of Glasgow, Scotland, UK

BEARPORT
PUBLISHING

New York, New York

Credits

Publisher: Kenn Goin
Senior Editor: Joyce Tavolacci
Creative Director: Spencer Brinker
Photo Researcher: Ruby Tuesday Books Ltd

Library of Congress Cataloging-in-Publication Data

Names: Owen, Ruth, 1967– author.
Title: Valley of the golden mummies : a giant cemetery / by Ruth Owen.
Other titles: Egypt's ancient secrets.
Description: New York, New York : Bearport Publishing Company, 2017. |
    Series: Egypt's ancient secrets | Includes bibliographical references and
    index.
Identifiers: LCCN 2016052126 (print) | LCCN 2016054952 (ebook) | ISBN
    9781684020249 (library) | ISBN 9781684020768 (ebook)
Subjects: LCSH: Bahariya Oasis (Egypt)—Antiquities—Juvenile literature. |
    Excavations (Archaeology)—Egypt—Bahariya Oasis—Juvenile literature. |
    Mummies—Egypt—Bahariya Oasis—Juvenile literature. |
    Mummies—Egypt—Juvenile literature. | Hawass, Zahi A.—Juvenile
    literature.
Classification: LCC DT73.B33 O94 2017 (print) | LCC DT73.B33 (ebook) | DDC
    932/.2—dc23
LC record available at https://lccn.loc.gov/2016052126

For more information, write to Bearport Publishing Company, Inc., 45 West 21st Street, Suite 3B, New York, New York 10010. Printed in the United States of America.

10 9 8 7 6 5 4 3 2

Contents

Eyes in the Sand

It was March 2, 1996. **Archaeologist** Zahi Hawass was **excavating** a skeleton in the Egyptian desert. Suddenly, two coworkers interrupted him. "We have found beautiful mummies," they said. At first, Hawass thought the men were joking. However, as they began describing the discovery, Hawass put down his tools and listened carefully.

A human skeleton buried in sand

Zahi Hawass (center) at work in the Egyptian desert

According to the workers, a local man named Abdul Maugoud had been riding his donkey in a desert valley near the Bahariya Oasis. All of a sudden, the animal stumbled into a hole. When Abdul looked down, he saw a shiny yellow face with lifelike eyes staring back at him. He had found an ancient Egyptian **tomb** containing a golden **mummy**!

Abdul Maugoud, who discovered the gold-covered mummy, with his donkey

An oasis is a place where underground water rises to the surface. The water allows trees and other plants to grow in a hot, dry desert. People often build villages around an oasis.

A Desert Cemetery

Hawass and his team rushed to investigate the discovery near the oasis. They soon confirmed that a huge ancient Egyptian **cemetery** was located there. Many tombs had been cut into the desert rock. Then, over the centuries, they had filled with sand and disappeared from view.

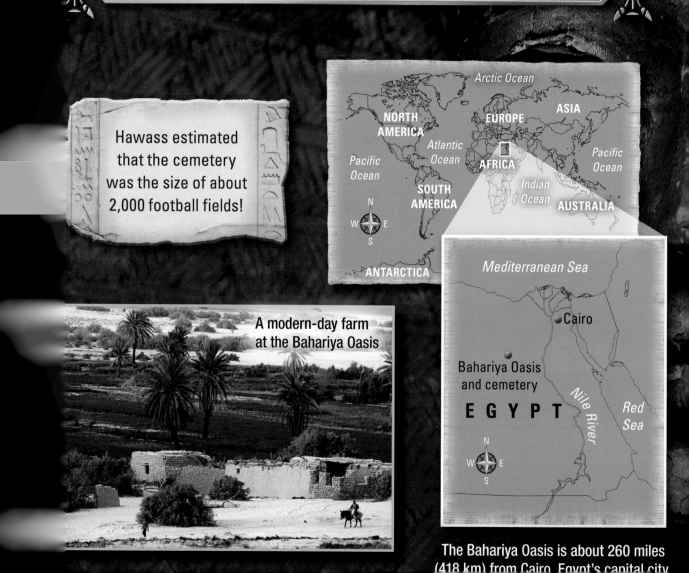

Hawass estimated that the cemetery was the size of about 2,000 football fields!

A modern-day farm at the Bahariya Oasis

Mediterranean Sea

Cairo

Bahariya Oasis and cemetery

E G Y P T

Nile River

Red Sea

The Bahariya Oasis is about 260 miles (418 km) from Cairo, Egypt's capital city

In 1999, Hawass and his team began excavating the first tomb they had found. As the archaeologists dug down into the sand, they found eight steps leading to a small room. Beyond this room, the team unearthed two burial chambers—both packed with mummies!

Zahi Hawass

One of the excavated burial chambers

Mummies

Excavating the Corpses

Inside the burial chamber, Hawass and his team discovered that the mummies were laid in niches, or shelflike spaces, cut into the rocky walls. Each niche was packed with sand. For days, the archaeologists shoveled it away. When they got closer to the mummies, they used smaller shovels, being extra careful not to harm the ancient **corpses**.

An archaeologist carefully brushes sand from a mummy in a niche.

Once a mummy was almost uncovered, workers used paintbrushes to gently brush away more sand. Finally, the team squeezed tools called blowers to puff away any remaining sand **particles** from the delicate mummies.

In total, Hawass and his team found 43 mummies in the first tomb. The archaeologists also excavated four other tombs. After just a few weeks of digging, they had found more than 100 mummies!

A brush and a blower

Hawass decided the first underground burial place probably belonged to one family. He believed **generations** of the same family had been laid to rest there over many decades.

The Golden Mummies

Hawass and his team discovered many different kinds of mummies in the tombs. The most spectacular were the golden mummies. These mummies were wrapped in **linen** bandages and wore golden masks and **chest plates**. The gold coverings were formed using a material called **cartonnage** made from linen and **plaster**. The cartonnage was then painted with a thin layer of melted gold. Because of all the valuable gold, Hawass thought that these mummies had probably been very wealthy people.

Gold mask

Linen bandages

Gold chest plate

To make cartonnage, moist layers of linen strips and plaster were laid on a mummy. Once the layers dried, the cartonnage hardened.

Other mummies had cartonnage masks and chest plates painted with colorful pictures of ancient Egyptian gods. These simpler, painted decorations suggested that the people were less wealthy.

Some of the mummies were wrapped in plain bandages with no masks or decorations. During their lives, Hawass guessed, these mummies were poorer members of **society**.

Gold mask

Painted cartonnage chest plate

Some of the mummies had eyes made of white glass and black rock. These lifelike eyes often startled archaeologists excavating the tombs.

The linen strips were wrapped around a mummy in different directions to form patterns of squares and diamonds. This image shows a mummy's bandaged feet.

Making a Mummy

Each of the corpses had been **preserved** before it was laid in its tomb. The ancient Egyptians believed that when someone died, he or she lived on in the **afterlife**. To do this, however, a person needed his or her body. So **embalmers** transformed a person's corpse into a mummy. Over the centuries, embalmers used different methods to make mummies.

Anubis

Mummy

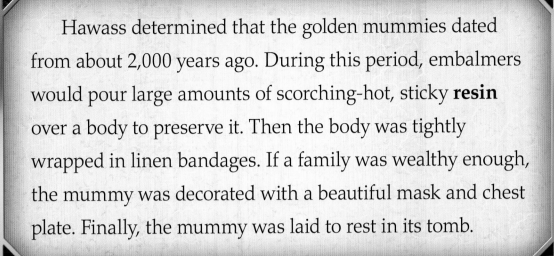

Hawass determined that the golden mummies dated from about 2,000 years ago. During this period, embalmers would pour large amounts of scorching-hot, sticky **resin** over a body to preserve it. Then the body was tightly wrapped in linen bandages. If a family was wealthy enough, the mummy was decorated with a beautiful mask and chest plate. Finally, the mummy was laid to rest in its tomb.

Clay statue of a mourner

The first tomb that was excavated at Bahariya contained four tiny clay statues of **mourners**. The statues were placed in the tomb to weep for the dead for all eternity.

The People of the Oasis

As Hawass and his team examined the mummies and their tombs, they found no names or other identifying marks. So who were the golden mummies?

The desert cemetery is close to the Bahariya Oasis. So the mummified people were probably residents of ancient villages in this area. Experts know that in ancient Egyptian times, the people who lived near the oasis grew grapes and dates for making wine.

Dates

Grapes

Pomegranate

Date palm trees

Ancient Egyptians made wine from grapes, dates, and pomegranates, as well as other fruits.

In ancient Egypt, people drank wine and gave it as gifts. Priests would also place wine in **temples** as an offering to the Egyptian gods. Jars of wine were even left in tombs for the dead to enjoy in the afterlife. Scientists believe that the golden mummies might have been wealthy landowners or **merchants** who sold wine. The mummies with simpler decorations were probably farmers who grew the grapes and dates.

Together for Eternity

Two of the most beautiful golden mummies found in the first tomb were most likely a married couple. Experts believe the husband and wife had been buried alongside each other so they could remain together in the afterlife. The female's mask was made to look as if it was smiling. Also, the mummy's head was slightly tilted toward her husband so she could lovingly gaze at him forever.

The mummy's curly hair is made of cartonnage that had been painted black.

On the male mummy's golden chest plate were images of the ancient Egyptian gods—Imsety, Duamutef, Hapi, and Qebehsenuef (kay-bay-SEN-oof). These gods were thought to protect the mummy's liver, stomach, lungs, and intestines. Some Egyptologists think the goddess Maat is also shown on the chest plate. She had an important part to play in a person's journey to the afterlife.

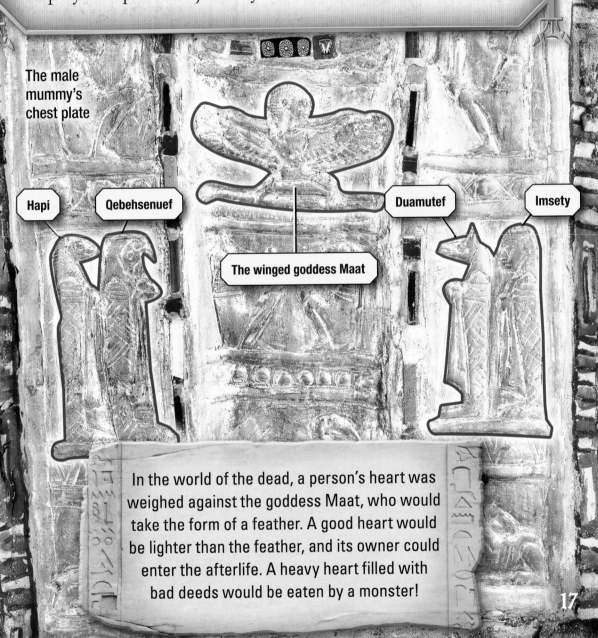

The male mummy's chest plate

Hapi

Qebehsenuef

The winged goddess Maat

Duamutef

Imsety

In the world of the dead, a person's heart was weighed against the goddess Maat, who would take the form of a feather. A good heart would be lighter than the feather, and its owner could enter the afterlife. A heavy heart filled with bad deeds would be eaten by a monster!

Mr. or Mrs. X?

As part of his investigations, Hawass decided to **X-ray** one of the mummies. He wanted to see inside its ancient wrappings to learn more about it. An X-ray can sometimes show archaeologists if the mummified person had any diseases, why he or she died, and how old the person was at the time of death.

In one of the tombs, Hawass found a single mummy alone in a niche. It had no mask or chest plate and was wrapped in plain bandages.

This is the mummy Hawass decided to X-ray. The person probably had no relatives and was one of the poorer residents of the Bahariya Oasis.

Hawass didn't know the sex of the mummy, so he called it Mr. or Mrs. X. He decided to send the mummy to a lab in the city of Cairo to be examined. Before the mummy could travel to Cairo, it was carefully covered with a special chemical. Once the substance dried, it would make the wrappings stronger and prevent them from unraveling or tearing.

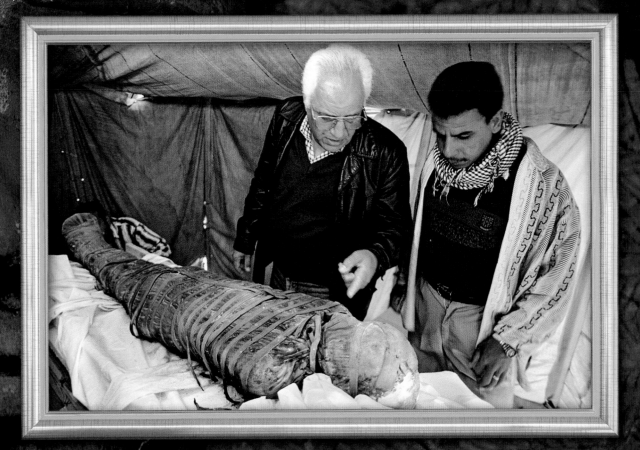

Even though Mr. or Mrs. X had been dead for around 2,000 years, Hawass and his team treated the mummy with great respect. Archaeologists never forget that a mummy was once a living person.

A Mummy Goes to Cairo

After centuries in the dark tomb, Mr. or Mrs. X was lifted into the bright sunlight. The mummy was carefully placed in a specially made wooden coffin and loaded onto a truck. The journey to Cairo took around eight hours. The driver traveled slowly to avoid bumps and potholes on the rough desert roads. It was very important that the mummy was not damaged during the trip.

The mummy is loaded onto a truck.

Finally, the mummy arrived safely in Cairo. The next morning, it underwent its examination. The results showed it was male. The scientists could see no signs of disease or figure out what had caused Mr. X's death. By looking at his bones and teeth, they could tell that Mr. X. was about 35 to 40 years old when he died.

Mr. X is prepared for his X-ray. The scientists discovered that he'd had two back teeth removed in his lifetime.

An American scientist named Teri Tucker discovered that many of the people in the Valley of the Golden Mummies were in their 20s or 30s when they died.

The Child Mummies

As Hawass continued his work in the Valley of the Golden Mummies, his team discovered two tiny child mummies. The little boy and girl were laid between their parents. Hawass decided to put the mummified children and their mother on display in a museum that had been built at the Bahariya Oasis. He would soon regret his decision, however.

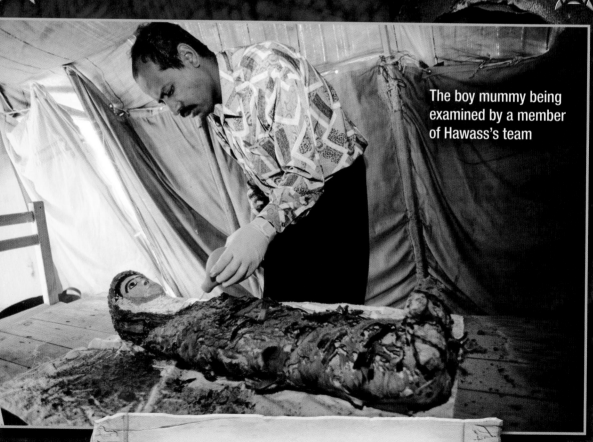

The boy mummy being examined by a member of Hawass's team

The child mummies were less than 3 feet (0.9 m) long. They were wrapped in linen bandages and had painted masks. The archaeologists guessed the children were around five years old.

After placing the mummies in the museum, Hawass began to have terrible nightmares. In his sleep, the child mummies seemed to come to life, their little arms stretching out to him. Then one night, Hawass dreamed that the tiny hands of the girl mummy were trying to strangle him! He woke up with a terrifying thought filling his head. When he'd moved the brother and sister mummies from their tomb, had he unleashed an ancient **curse**?

An archaeologist uncovers the little girl mummy.

The Ancient Curse

So is there any truth to the ancient curse? In the 1800s, explorers and archaeologists began to visit Egypt to look for ancient tombs. Stories soon grew about a curse that would strike down any person who dared enter a tomb or disturb a mummy. When Zahi Hawass began to experience terrifying nightmares, he wondered if the child mummies had cursed him.

Archaeologists have found curses carved at the entrances of tombs. Ancient Egyptians knew that robbers might try to steal treasures from tombs, so these warnings were likely a way to keep intruders out.

Crocodile

Hippo

Lion

A curse outside this tomb warns against entering, and even claims that anyone who damages or disturbs the tomb will be eaten by crocodiles, hippopotamuses, and lions!

Exhausted from lack of sleep, Hawass went over every detail of the day his team had moved the mummies from their tomb. Suddenly, he realized what was wrong. The father of the child mummies had been left behind in the desert. Hawass arranged for the father mummy to be reunited with his family at the museum. The child mummies never disturbed Hawass's sleep again!

The girl and boy mummies wrapped in linen at the museum

10,000 Mummies!

In addition to the mummies, many other ancient **artifacts** were discovered in the tombs at the Bahariya cemetery. These objects were placed alongside the mummies so they would have some of their belongings in the afterlife. The tombs contained jewelry made of copper, ivory, glass, and **gemstones**. Jars of wine, cups, dishes, and cooking pots were also found. Even a toy horse made of clay was excavated near the child mummies.

Hawass has estimated that there could be as many as 10,000 mummies—and many more ancient objects—still buried in the vast desert cemetery. To excavate all the tombs will take decades. For now, the undiscovered mummies and their tombs remain hidden beneath the sand. Only time will tell what ancient secrets the Valley of the Golden Mummies still has to reveal.

An archaeologist examines skulls lying in the desert near Bahariya Oasis.

Archaeologists have found many skulls and other human bones in the desert sand. These bones were once buried underground but rose to the surface when the sand blew away or wild animals dug them up.

27

Egypt's Ancient Secrets

Zahi Hawass and his team uncovered many ancient secrets at the desert cemetery . . . but some mysteries still remain.

What Happened to the Bride Mummy?

In one of the tombs, the team found the mummy of a young woman. She was wearing a headdress, and her mask was painted white with rosy cheeks. The archaeologists believe the mummy was made to look like a bride. They think she probably died before her wedding day. How did the young bride-to-be die? And who was she?

The Bride Mummy

Did the Child Mummies Really Curse Hawass?

Excavating tombs and investigating their contents costs a lot of money. One way to raise money is to put mummies and other artifacts on display in museums. Perhaps Zahi Hawass, without realizing it, felt guilty about removing the child mummies from their tomb and placing them in a museum. Or maybe the dead children really did reach out from the afterlife to be reunited with their father.

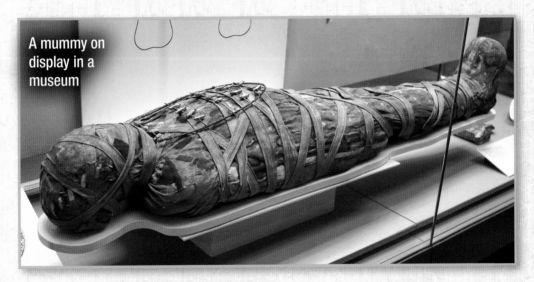

A mummy on display in a museum

Could Bahariya Contain the Tomb of an Ancient Ruler?

The golden mummies found at the Bahariya Oasis were probably wealthy members of society. However, could someone even more important still lie beneath the sand? Maybe a governor or an army commander is buried in the desert. What beautiful decorations might be found on the mummy of such an imporant person?

Glossary

afterlife (AF-tur-life) the life a person has after he or she dies

archaeologist (ar-kee-OL-uh-jist) a scientist who learns about ancient times by studying things he or she digs up, such as tombs, old buildings, and tools

artifacts (ART-uh-fakts) objects that were made by people

cartonnage (KAR-ton-naj) a hard substance made of linen and plaster that was used for making masks and other coverings for mummies

cemetery (SEM-uh-ter-ee) an area of land where dead bodies are buried

chest plates (CHEST PLEYTS) decorative, vestlike coverings on a mummy's chest

corpses (KORPS-iz) dead bodies

curse (KURSS) something that brings or causes evil or misfortune

embalmers (em-BALHM-urz) people who prepare dead bodies for burial

excavating (*eks*-kuh-VAYT-ing) uncovering or digging up an archaeological site

gemstones (JEM-stohns) precious or semi-precious stones that have been cut, shaped, and polished for use in jewelry

generations (jen-uh-RAY-shuhnz) groups of people born around the same time

linen (LIN-uhn) cloth that's made by weaving the fibers of flax plants

merchants (MUR-chuhnts) people who buy and sell goods

mourners (MOHRN-urz) people who grieve for a dead person and often attend his or her funeral

mummy (MUH-mee) the preserved body of a dead person or animal

particles (PAR-tuh-kuhlz) tiny pieces of something, such as rock

plaster (PLASS-tur) a mixture of water and tiny bits of rock that hardens as it dries

preserved (pri-ZURVD) treated something to stop it from rotting

resin (REZ-in) a thick, sticky substance often obtained from trees

society (suh-SYE-uh-tee) all the people who live in the same country or area and share the same laws and customs

temples (TEM-puhlz) religious buildings where people worship

tomb (TOOM) a grave, room, or building in which a dead body is placed

X-ray (EKS-ray) to take photographs of the inside of a person's body

Bibliography

Hawass, Zahi. *Valley of the Golden Mummies.* Cairo, Egypt: The American University in Cairo Press (2000).

Taylor, John H., and Daniel Antoine. *Ancient Lives, New Discoveries: Eight Mummies, Eight Stories.* London: The British Museum Press (2014).

Read More

Gifford, Clive. *Tomb Hunters: Discover the Incredible Lost World of Egypt (Trailblazers).* Philadelphia: Running Press Kids (2007).

Hall, Brianna. *Mummies of Ancient Egypt (Fact Finders).* North Mankato, MN: Capstone Press (2012).

Owen, Ruth. *How to Make an Egyptian Mummy (It's a Fact!).* New York: Ruby Tuesday Books (2015).

Learn More Online

To learn more about the Valley of the Golden Mummies, visit
www.bearportpublishing.com/EgyptsAncientSecrets

Index

About the Author

Ruth Owen has written many nonfiction books for children. She has always been fascinated by ancient Egyptian history and the work of archaeologists.